TOUCHDOWN TRIVIA

Secrets, statistics, and little-known facts about football

Bruce Adelson

illustrations by Harry Pulver Jr.

Lerner Publications Company • Minneapolis

9251356

For Sharon Craig, Vicki Fagliarone, Laurie Goss, Sally Keyes, Jan McConnel, and Lorraine Nasiatka—second grade teachers at Zachary Taylor Elementary School in Arlington, Virginia. Your dedication, collegiality, and professionalism will inspire me for years to come. Thank you.

—B.A.

Thank you to Tricia Trilli of the Pro Football Hall of Fame in Canton, Ohio, for her help in researching this book. The assistance of Megan Cifrino, Elizabeth Crutsinger, Lily Gallindo, and Jay Lama of Joan Yocum's fifth grade language arts class at Zachary Taylor Elementary School is gratefully acknowledged. Your exuberance and helpful review of this book contributed to its completion. Thanks as well to Joan Yocum, whose enthusiasm for our writing project will always be appreciated.

Illustrations by Harry Pulver Jr.
Book design and electronic prepress: Steve Foley, Mike Kohn, Sean Todd

This book is available in two editions:
Library binding by Lerner Publications Company
Soft cover by First Avenue Editions
241 First Avenue North, Minneapolis, Minnesota 55401

Library of Congress Cataloging-in-Publication Data

Adelson, Bruce.
    Touchdown trivia / by Bruce Adelson ; illustrations by Harry Pulver Jr.
    p.   cm. (sports trivia)
    Includes bibliographical references (p.) and index.
    Summary: Presents facts and figures about the game of football—past and present, and particularly about professional play in the NFL.
    ISBN 0-8225-3312-x (hardcover : alk. paper). — ISBN 0-8225-9805-1 (pbk. : alk. paper) 1. Football-Miscellanea-Juvenile literature. [1. Football-Miscellanea.] I. Pulver, Harry, ill. II. Title.
    GV950.7.A34 1998
    796.332-dc21   97-46447

Manufactured in the United States of America
1 2 3 4 5 6 - JR - 03 02 01 00 99 98

Contents

Chapter 1

The Game of Football

Did You Know?

The sport of football was first played in eleventh-century England. People in neighboring villages played a game in which they kicked hard objects—like rocks and human skulls—around the large fields that separated the communities from one another. After awhile, the early football players began using a softer ball, typically an inflated cow bladder.

An 1885 woodcutting shows a football player kicking the ball.

The modern sport of football started out as a kicking game. Football originally grew out of the games of soccer and rugby. Because the ball was kicked, the sport was appropriately called football. The game of soccer is also called football in many countries, but throughout the United States, Canada, and a few other nations, football is American football.

Early American football games, which looked more like soccer matches, were first played by college teams in the 1860s. Professional football did not begin until the 1890s.

By 1876, a distinct game of American football, complete with its own set of rules, had been invented. This early version of football resembled rugby more than soccer since the players ran with the ball instead of just kicking it. The ball also was egg shaped, looking more like the pointed ball used in rugby than the round one used in soccer. Early football players could only run with or kick the ball. Passing was not allowed until 1906.

The first football players wore plain street clothes instead of uniforms. When Rutgers and Princeton Universities played the first college football game in the United States in 1869, the players just took off their hats, coats, and vests and played the game in street clothes. Five years later, when Harvard and McGill Universities played a football game, the first uniforms appeared—the Harvard players wore sweaters and tied handkerchiefs around their heads, while McGill's players wore white pants, striped jerseys, and turbans.

Princeton University's team was the first to wear a complete uniform. In an 1876 football game against the

Pudge Heffelfinger

Did You Know?

On November 12, 1892, William "Pudge" Heffelfinger became the first professional football player. Heffelfinger was paid $500 by his team, the Allegheny Athletic Association, for playing in a game against the Pittsburgh Athletic Club. Many sports historians say that in 1893, the Pittsburgh AC signed Grant Dibert to the first professional contract for a whole football season.

University of Pennsylvania, Princeton football players sported black knee pants, stockings, and black jerseys with orange stripes and an orange P. They also wore baseball shoes and caps. But their jerseys had no numbers on the back. Uniform numbers did not appear until 1908.

Unlike modern football players, who wear lots of different pads to protect themselves from getting hurt, the earliest players did not wear any padding. Many players felt that wearing protective pads made them look silly. They preferred to play the rough and tough game of football without any protection at all. These players gradually changed their minds about padding after seeing how many early players were seriously injured and even killed from the battering they received during football games.

Patented Outside Pads.
Pat. No. 759,833.

S. & D. Patented Outside Pads.

1234 Material used in this suit guaranteed to be the best quality of moleskin obtainable. The hips, knees and shoulders have our latest patent outside pads with hair stuffing, and the thighs have outside cane strips. Pant and jacket are connected by a substantial elastic belt. Notice style of jackets we are using in these suits. Suit, **$8 00**

1235 Material used in this suit is of second grade of moleskin, made same as 1234. Suit.. **7 00**

1236 Material used in this suit is of genuine army khaki, tan color, made same as 1234. Suit..................... .... **5 50**

Patented Outside Pads.
Pat. No. 759,833.

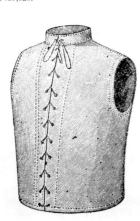

Pads were not used at all until the 1890s, when shin guards and shoulder pads made from curled horsehair appeared in football games. In 1909 shoulder pads made from leather and asbestos and shaped a little like those used today were invented. Modern players wear shoulder, thigh, knee, shin, forearm, elbow, and even kidney pads, made usually from foam and plastic.

Did You Know?

Early football uniforms were not very colorful, and they did not have any team logos or names on them. The first professional team with its name on a uniform was the Green Bay Packers. In 1921 this team was sponsored by the Indian Packing Company and wore jerseys with the words "Acme Packers" printed on the front. In 1926, the Duluth (Minnesota) Eskimos became the first team with its own logo. Players wore uniforms with a black and white igloo printed on the front of each one.

Trivia Teaser #1

Are footballs really made of pigskin?

Turn to page 57 for the answer.

Besides not wanting to wear padding, early football players did not wear helmets. For head protection, they relied on stocking caps and long hair. Yale University football players refused to get haircuts during the summer of 1890 so they would have long hair to protect their heads during the upcoming football season.

The first football helmet was invented in 1896 by George "Rose" Barclay, a player for Lafayette College in Pennsylvania. With the help of a horse harness maker, Barclay sewed three thick leather straps into a tightly fitting headpiece for a game against the University of Pennsylvania.

The first football game featuring a player with a helmet

Just one of these four early football players chose to wear a helmet.

almost did not take place. Officials debated whether the rules permitted players to wear headgear like Barclay's. But after a lot of discussion, the officials did allow George Barclay to wear the football helmet.

For the most part, football players resisted wearing helmets. Coaches believed that headgear made from any material heavier than cloth would slow players down. But eventually, everyone in football became used to the idea of wearing helmets as a way of avoiding serious injury and death while playing the game. By 1907 there were five different styles of headgear for players to choose from. Early helmets were mostly made from different types of leather and did not have face masks. Football helmets became an accepted part of football uniforms in the 1930s. Plastic helmets became popular in the 1950s, when face masks also first appeared.

Left: A player in a 1930s helmet. Above: Players in 1950s-style helmets with face masks.

Modern NFL helmets are much different from the earlier ones. These days helmets are scientifically designed. Each player's head is measured and fitted with a headpiece. Each helmet is equipped with a foam stabilizer system and is pumped up with air to provide an extra layer of head protection. In 1994 radios were installed inside helmets worn by NFL quarterbacks, allowing them to hear instructions from coaches on the sidelines.

Did You Know?

Darryl Johnston, fullback for the Dallas Cowboys, wears a helmet, shoulder pads, and other padding weighing 33 pounds. But kickers and punters, who usually are not involved in tackling or hitting other players, need less gear than Johnston, so their equipment weighs only about 15 pounds.

Which National Football League club is the oldest in professional football?

A. New York Giants
B. Washington Redskins
C. Detroit Lions
D. Arizona Cardinals

Turn the page for the answer.

A: **D. Arizona Cardinals.** The Cardinals are the oldest continually operating pro football team. In 1899, the Morgan Athletic Club played football on the south side of Chicago. This team later became known as the Normals. After borrowing cardinal red jerseys from the University of Chicago in 1922, the team was nicknamed the Cardinals. This name stuck, and over the years, the club has been known as the Racine Cardinals, Chicago Cardinals, St. Louis Cardinals, Phoenix Cardinals, and the Arizona Cardinals.

Over the years, the game of football has changed along with players' uniforms. Today's players are bigger and faster than many of the earliest players. One of the biggest differences between modern NFL football and earlier versions is that players used to play both offense and defense during each game. Although Deion Sanders of the Dallas Cowboys occasionally plays on both offense and on defense—as wide receiver and cornerback—all football players used to participate in every play of the game. This mode of play lasted until the late 1950s, when players specialized in either an offensive or defensive position.

Chuck Bednarik of the Philadelphia Eagles was the last NFL player to play both offensive and defensive positions in every game. He played center and linebacker. Although he had stopped playing linebacker in 1957, he returned to being a two-way player in 1960 when his teammates' injuries led him to help out by again playing both linebacker and center. In his 14-year NFL career, Bednarik missed only one game, playing in a total of 256. Bednarik is a member of the Pro Football Hall of Fame.

Chuck Bednarik scores a touchdown.

Did You Know?

The goal posts in National Football League stadiums used to be in the end zone, only 6 feet behind the goal line. Their position on the playing field caused problems—players would hit them while running full speed to the end zone. The NFL moved the goal posts out of the end zone in 1974.

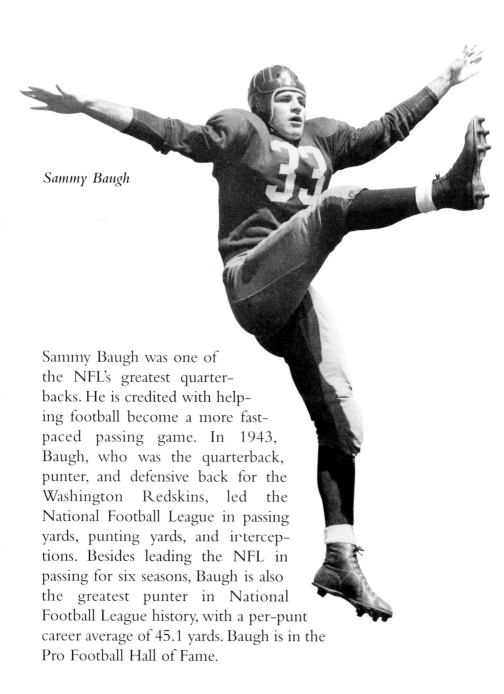

Sammy Baugh

Sammy Baugh was one of the NFL's greatest quarterbacks. He is credited with helping football become a more fast-paced passing game. In 1943, Baugh, who was the quarterback, punter, and defensive back for the Washington Redskins, led the National Football League in passing yards, punting yards, and interceptions. Besides leading the NFL in passing for six seasons, Baugh is also the greatest punter in National Football League history, with a per-punt career average of 45.1 yards. Baugh is in the Pro Football Hall of Fame.

Trivia Teaser #2

I have played 14 seasons in the National Football League. I am the only quarterback in NFL history to pass for 50,000 yards in my career. I have also completed more passes and thrown more touchdowns than any other quarterback. I play for a team in the Eastern Division of the NFL's American Football Conference. Who am I?

Chapter 2

African Americans and Football

Did You Know?

The history of black football players goes back to the nineteenth century. At that time, African Americans played for several colleges. The 1889 Amherst College football squad was one of the first on which blacks and whites played together.

In the early years of football, blacks and whites played together on several college and amateur teams. African Americans also formed several teams of their own. But there were no professional African American football players until 1904. On September 15 of that year, Charles Follis signed a football contract with the Shelby (Ohio) Blues. He had played for Shelby since 1902 as an amateur.

One of Follis's teammates in 1902 and 1903 was named Branch Rickey. In 1947 Rickey made history in baseball, when he brought Jackie Robinson onto the Brooklyn Dodgers team, making Robinson the first African American to play major league baseball in the twentieth century.

In his first game as a professional football player, Follis ran for an 83-yard touchdown, as Shelby defeated a team from Marion, Ohio, 29–0. During Shelby's first 10 games in 1904, the Blues scored 317 points and gave up only 28.

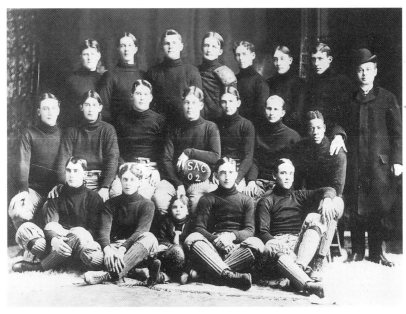

Charles Follis (middle row, far right) poses with the Shelby team.

Just like Jackie Robinson in baseball, Charles Follis was treated differently by some of the players and fans because he was black. During one game in Toledo, Ohio, some fans shouted racial insults at Follis. The taunting continued until Jack Tattersoll—Toledo's quarterback, team captain, and a white man—intervened. Tattersoll told the fans that Follis was a gentleman and a great player and that they should not call him names because of his skin color. The Toledo fans applauded the words of their team's captain and stopped abusing Follis.

Unfortunately, Follis encountered discrimination and racism in other places, including his hometown of Shelby. When Follis and his teammates went to a restaurant after practice one day, the restaurant's owner forced Follis to leave, saying he only served food to white people.

Follis was a very gifted athlete. Nicknamed the Black Cyclone because of his great speed, Follis went on to play professional baseball after his football career ended due to an injury in 1906. He played for the Cuban Giants from 1907 to 1910.

Did You Know?

Fewer than two dozen African Americans have played quarterback in the history of the National Football League. Willie Thrower became the first black NFL quarterback in 1953, when he played for the Chicago Bears. Jeff Blake is another African American quarterback who plays for the Cincinnati Bengals.

Willie Thrower

After Charles Follis ended his career, other African Americans continued to play football. From 1920 to 1933, 12 black men played professional football. But in 1933, only two African Americans, Joe Lillard and Raymond Kemp, remained in the NFL. After 1933, National Football League teams refused to sign black players. There was an agreement among team owners that no blacks would be allowed to play football in the National Football League. Despite the NFL's ban, African Americans still wanted to play football. Since they could not play in the National Football League, they formed their own leagues in the 1930s. Black football leagues operated until the mid–1940s.

African Americans were not allowed to play professional football with white players until March 1946, when the Los Angeles Rams signed Kenny Washington, making him the first black player in the NFL since 1933. Later that year, pro football teams signed three other African American players. Woody Strode signed a contract with the Rams, and Bill Willis and Marion Motley were signed by the Cleveland Browns. At the time, the Browns played in the All–American Football Conference, a professional football league that went out of business in 1950. Marion Motley and Bill Willis are members of Pro Football's Hall of Fame.

Left: Marion Motley
Above: Kenny Washington

These African American athletes often had to deal with prejudiced fans and players. In the 1940s, 1950s, and 1960s, some parts of the United States were segregated. In segregated cities, blacks were not allowed to eat in white restaurants or sleep in the same hotels as whites. African American athletes had to sleep and eat apart from their teammates, in places where the only customers were black people.

Over time, the National Football League became more accepting of African Americans who wanted to join the league. In 1965 Burl Toler was hired as a field judge by the NFL, becoming the first black official in professional football. This occurred one year before major league baseball hired its first African American umpire, Emmett Ashford. In 1988, Johnny Grier became the NFL's first black referee. More than 60 percent of the players in the National Football League are African American.

Why doesn't any NFL quarterback have a uniform number over 20? Why do all wide receivers have very high numbers?

A: ***Beginning with the 1952 NFL season, the league passed a rule requiring that players at each position must wear certain numbers to help officials keep track of where players were supposed to be on the field.*** Here is a list of numbers for each position on an NFL team:

Quarterbacks and Kickers: 1–19
Defensive Backs and Running Backs: 20–49
Linebackers and Centers: 50–59
Defensive and Offensive Linemen: 60–79 or 90–99
Wide Receivers and Tight Ends: 80–89

Who was the first African American quarterback to win the Super Bowl?

Which running back holds the record for the most career rushing yards in National Football League history?

A. Emmitt Smith

B. Walter Payton

C. Jim Brown

D. Tony Dorsett

A: **B. Walter Payton.** In his 13-year NFL career with the Chicago Bears, Walter Payton gained 16,726 yards and scored 110 career touchdowns. In 77 games, Payton gained at least 100 yards. All of these were NFL records. On November 20, 1977, Walter Payton set an all-time record when he gained 275 rushing yards in a game against the Minnesota Vikings.

Trivia Teaser #4

I am an NFL running back. I won the Heisman Trophy in 1988, when I played college football for the University of Oklahoma. In my rookie year in the National Football League, I led the league with 1,470 rushing yards. I have played eight years in the NFL. From 1989 to 1995, I gained more rushing yards than any other current NFL running back. I play for a team in the NFL's National Football Conference. Who am I?

Chapter 3

Women and Football

Although it may seem that football is a sport just for men, women have played football for most of the twentieth century. A Columbus, Ohio, newspaper reported that on November 18, 1903, a football game between two teams of high school-age girls took place. Since then, women have been involved with football at many different levels.

Since the early 1970s, many young women throughout the United States have played high school football. Kari McCallum followed a family tradition and became a high school football player in Seattle, Washington. Kari was the second-string kicker for her varsity team. Her three brothers had played on the same team before she did. In 1987, Heidi Kaiser became the first girl to score a point in a Florida high school football game. She kicked six extra points in one game and two extra points and a field goal in the next one. While many girls have been the punters or kickers for their teams, more and more young women are playing other positions, too. For example, Rachel Seymour played defensive and offensive end for Fairbanks Lathrop High School in Alaska.

Anna Lakovitch was a kicker for the Pine Crest High School football team in Boca Raton, Florida, in 1996.

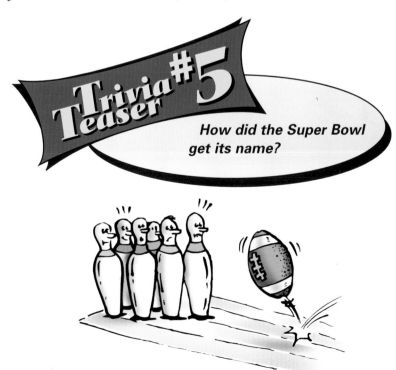

Trivia Teaser #5

How did the Super Bowl get its name?

Women have also played professional football in many places, from the United States to Japan. In 1965 the Women's Professional Football League (WPFL) was formed. WPFL teams hailed from Cleveland, Cincinnati, Akron, Buffalo, Pittsburgh, and several other cities. The league folded in 1974, after the National Women's Football League (NWFL) was founded. This league had 10 teams with several in large cities such as Dallas, Detroit, San Diego, and Houston. The NWFL played games according to National Football League rules with only small differences.

Pat Palinkas was the first female to play pro football with the men. In 1970 she played for the Orlando (Florida) Panthers in a game against the Bridgeport (Connecticut) Jets. Both teams played in the Atlantic Coast League, a pro football minor league. Palinkas was the extra-point and field-goal holder for the Panthers' kicker. In 1972, Nancy Witt, the owner of a minor league football team in Colorado, played for her team as the holder on field goal attempts.

Did You Know?

In 1979 Georgia Frontiere became the first woman to own a National Football League team, when she gained control of the Los Angeles Rams. Known for her outspoken character and hands-on style, Frontiere moved the Rams to St. Louis, Missouri, in 1995. Since Frontiere has owned the Rams, the team has played in one Super Bowl (XIV).

Over the years, one player has stood out as probably the finest woman ever to play pro football. Linda Jefferson, 5 feet 4 inches tall and 130 pounds, played professional football in the 1970s and 1980s as a running back for the Toledo Troopers of the National Women's Football League.

In her career, Jefferson gained more than 8,000 rushing yards and scored 140 touchdowns. Jefferson also gained at

Linda Jefferson

least 1,000 yards per season for six seasons. In 1975 Jefferson gained 1,357 yards and scored 14 touchdowns and was named Woman Athlete of the Year by *WomenSports* magazine.

Helped by their star player, Toledo was undefeated in its first 28 games and lost only once in 56 contests. During a 37–12 victory over the Dallas Bluebonnets, Jefferson scored 5 touchdowns and gained 209 yards on only 10 carries, an incredible average of more than 20 yards per rushing attempt.

Besides playing football, women have been involved with the sport as team owners, reporters, and broadcasters. In

1987, Gayle Sierens became the first woman to broadcast an NFL game on network television. She was one of the announcers for a contest between the Seattle Seahawks and Kansas City Chiefs.

Gayle Sierens talked with statistician Elliot Kalb (left) before Sierens broadcasted an NFL game between the Seattle Seahawks and the Kansas City Chiefs.

Hannah Storm

Leslie Visser

 *Who was the first woman to play college football, and when did she play?*

Liz Heaston became the first woman to play in an intercollegiate football game in 1997. Playing for Willamette College (Oregon), she kicked two extra points in a game against Linfield College. Willamette won the game 27–0. Heaston also played soccer for Willamette. Before Heaston played college football, other women had practiced but had never played in any official games.

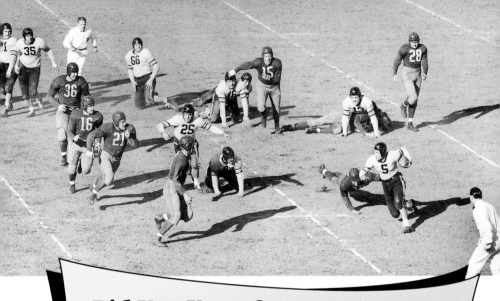

Did You Know?

One of football's most famous games was the 1940 NFL Championship between the Chicago Bears and Washington Redskins. In a game three weeks before the championship, Washington defeated Chicago 7–3. After this game was over, several Redskins made fun of the Bears. They called them "cry babies" and "quitters." On November 17, 1940, these two teams played again. But the second game was very different than the first one. The Bears remembered what the Redskins had said about them. Chicago scored a touchdown in the first 55 seconds of the game and led Washington 28–0 at halftime. By the end of the game, Chicago—led by quarterback Sid Luckman—had scored 11 touchdowns. After the Bears scored their last two touchdowns, the Redskins asked them not to kick any more extra points after scoring touchdowns because the Redskins had run out of footballs. The final score: Chicago 73, Washington 0.

Chapter 4

Statistics

Rushing yards, receiving yards, passing yards, and net yards are four of football's most important statistics. They can be figured out by keeping track of how many yards a player gains each season.

Many people think that Jerry Rice of the San Francisco 49ers is the greatest wide receiver in NFL history. His receiving yards statistic can help show why. In 12 seasons, Rice caught 1,050 passes for 16,377 yards. He is the only NFL wide receiver to ever gain 15,000 career yards.

By dividing Rice's yards (16,377) by the number of passes he caught (1,050), we see that he gained an average of 15.597 yards (rounded to 15.60) on each pass he caught. This figure, 15.60, is called Rice's average gain per pass reception.

Jerry Rice

Art Monk

Compare Rice's statistics to Art Monk's. Monk caught 940 passes, the second most in history, in his NFL career. Monk also gained 12,721 yards. Figure out Monk's average gain per pass reception.

$$12{,}721 \div 940 = 13.53$$

Art Monk was a great wide receiver. How do his statistics compare to Jerry Rice's? Rice has gained almost 4,000 yards more than Art ($16{,}377 - 12{,}721 = 3{,}656$) while catching only 110 more passes. Rice also gains about two yards more than Monk did for each pass reception ($15.60 - 13.53 = 2.07$). As with most statistics, a minimum number of yards covered (3,500) must be achieved by a receiver to compare that receiver's stats with those of another player.

Trivia Teaser #6

I am the quarterback for a team in the Western Division of the NFL's American Football Conference. I have led my team to four Super Bowls, winning in 1998. I am well known for scoring winning touchdowns at the ends of games. I have done this more than 30 times in my career.
I am also the only NFL quarterback to have signed a professional baseball contract with the New York Yankees. Who am I?

Did You Know?

On September 28, 1951, Norm van Brocklin, quarterback for the Los Angeles Rams, had the greatest passing game in NFL history. Van Brocklin passed for 554 yards, threw 5 touchdown passes, and helped the Rams defeat the New York Yanks 54–14. Norm van Brocklin is in the Pro Football Hall of Fame.

Rams quarterback Norm van Brocklin throws a pass.

Running backs gain yardage by running with the football toward the opposing team's goal line. There have been many great running backs in NFL history. Walter Payton gained more yards than any other running back, but Jim Brown is considered by many to be the greatest running back to ever play in the NFL. Let's see why.

Walter Payton

Jim Brown

	Years in NFL	Rushing attempts	Yards gained
Payton	13	3,838	16,726
Brown	9	2,359	12,312

To compare how good these players were, we must look closely at their stats. Let's figure out their average yards gained each time they carried the ball. To do this, we divide yards gained by rushing attempts. For Walter Payton:

$$16{,}726 \div 3{,}838 = 4.357 \ (4.36)$$

For Jim Brown:

$$12{,}312 \div 2{,}359 = 5.219 \ (5.22)$$

What about the average number of yards they gained each season? To figure this out, we divide again—the number of yards gained by the number of years in the NFL. For Walter Payton:

$$16{,}726 \div 13 = 1{,}230$$

For Jim Brown:

$$12{,}312 \div 9 = 1{,}368$$

Brown's averages are greater than Payton's. That's why, although both men were great players and both are in Pro Football's Hall of Fame, many think Jim Brown was the greatest running back, even though Walter Payton holds the record for most rushing yards gained in an NFL career.

Jim Brown rushes for some yards.

Trivia Teaser #7

In 1996, which two NFL running backs had the best statistic for average yards gained per carry?

Quarterbacks gain yardage when receivers catch their passes. To get an idea of how good a quarterback is, we take a look at the statistics. Otto Graham and Len Dawson are two of the greatest quarterbacks in football history. They are both members of Pro Football's Hall of Fame.

Otto Graham

Len Dawson

Len Dawson played 19 years of pro football for the Kansas City Chiefs. He gained 28,711 passing yards by completing 2,136 passes. Figure out the average yardage gain for each of Dawson's pass completions by dividing passing yards by completed passes.

$$28{,}711 \div 2{,}136 = 13.44$$

Otto Graham played 11 years of pro football, mostly for the Cleveland Browns. He gained 23,584 passing yards by completing 1,464 passes. Dawson completed almost 700 more passes than Graham, and he also gained more total yardage. But what was Graham's average gain per pass completion?

$$23{,}584 \div 1{,}464 = 16.10$$

Although Dawson completed more passes and gained more yards than Graham, Graham gained almost 3 yards more each time he completed a pass.

Did You Know?

Fran Tarkenton, an 18-year pro quarterback who played 13 seasons with the Minnesota Vikings, originated the quarterback scramble. Faced with an offensive line that had trouble blocking the defense, Tarkenton often kept plays alive by dodging and darting to avoid defenders behind the line of scrimmage until a receiver or a running play opened up. During his career, Tarkenton amassed more than 50,000 yards, passing for 342 touchdowns and rushing for 32 touchdowns.

Which NFL quarterback has won more play-off games and gained more passing yards in the playoffs than any quarterback in history?

A. Troy Aikman

B. Terry Bradshaw

C. Joe Montana

D. Steve Young

A: **C. Joe Montana.** In his 16-year NFL career with the San Francisco 49ers and Kansas City Chiefs, Montana won 17 of the 23 playoff games he played in. He also holds the NFL record for most passing yards gained (5,772) in the play-offs. With the 49ers, Montana played on four Super Bowl Champion teams, in 1981, 1984, 1988, and 1989.

Walter Payton

Net yardage is the total amount of yards a player gains by catching passes, returning kickoffs, and rushing. Walter Payton has more net yards than any other player in football history, with 16,726 rushing yards, 4,538 pass-receiving yards, and 539 kickoff return yards. To figure out net yardage, add the totals for these three stats.

$$\begin{array}{r} 16{,}726 \\ 4{,}538 \\ +\ \ 539 \\ \hline 21{,}803 \end{array}$$

Trivia Teaser #8

How did the football term
"quarterback sack" get its name?

Did You Know?

The NFL championship game between the Dallas Cowboys and Green Bay Packers on December 31, 1967, is known as the "Ice Bowl" because of the cold weather that day in Green Bay. The temperature was -13° F and there was also a strong wind blowing, making it the coldest New Year's Eve in Green Bay history. The air was so cold that many players' hands were numb. The referee and other officials on the field were shaking because of the cold. Before the game, they had convinced the owner of a sporting goods store to open early to sell them ear muffs, thermal underwear, and extra socks. But they were still cold! The officials' whistles did not even work because the little balls inside them had frozen and stuck. With 16 seconds left in the game and Dallas winning 17–14, Green Bay had the ball on the Dallas 1-yard line. The Packers' quarterback, Bart Starr, surprised the Cowboys by running a quarterback sneak over the goal line to score the winning touchdown. Green Bay won 21–17. Two weeks later, the Packers defeated the Oakland Raiders to win Super Bowl II.

Bart Starr lies in the middle of a hogpile after scoring the winning touchdown in the 1967 NFL championship game.

Chapter 5

Football's Best Players

Over the years, the statistics of every National Football League player have been recorded. Here is a list of football's greatest players and some of their most important statistics. The top five players with the most rushing yards, most passing yards, most receiving yards, most net yards, and most touchdowns in football history are listed. The stats of some of the best current NFL players are also included, so you can see how your favorites match up against football's all-time best players. Your knowledge of football statistics will help you compare players to find out who are the best in history.

Most Rushing Yards

Walter Payton	16,726
Eric Dickerson	13,259
Tony Dorsett	12,739
Jim Brown	12,312
Franco Harris	12,120

Players of the '90s

Marcus Allen	11,738
Barry Sanders	11,725
Thurman Thomas	10,762
Emmitt Smith	10,160
Herschel Walker	8,205

Walter Payton

Dan Marino

Most Passing Touchdowns

Dan Marino	385
Fran Tarkenton	342
Johnny Unitas	290
Joe Montana	273
Dave Krieg	261

Players of the '90s

Dan Marino	385
Warren Moon	279
John Elway	278
Dave Krieg	261
Boomer Esiason	257

Most Passing Yards

Dan Marino	51,636
Fran Tarkenton	47,003
John Elway	45,034
Warren Moon	43,787
Dan Fouts	43,040

Players of the '90s

Boomer Esiason	36,442
Jim Kelly	35,467
Steve Young	29,581
Brett Favre	18,724
Jim Harbaugh	14,212

Brett Favre

Most Receiving Touchdowns

Jerry Rice	155
Steve Largent	100
Cris Carter	89
Don Maynard	88
Andre Reed	80

Players of the '90s

Jerry Rice	155
Cris Carter	89
Andre Reed	80
Irving Fryer	75
Andre Rizen	73

Jerry Rice

Cris Carter

Most Receiving Yards

Jerry Rice	16,377
James Lofton	14,004
Henry Ellard	13,177
Steve Largent	13,089
Art Monk	12,721

Players of the '90s

Henry Ellard	13,177
Andre Reed	10,884
Brett Perriman	6,197
Herman Moore	6,191
Isaac Bruce	3,391

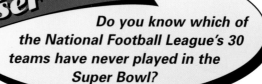

Trivia #9 Teaser

Do you know which of
the National Football League's 30
teams have never played in the
Super Bowl?

Walter Payton

Emmitt Smith

Most Net Yards

Walter Payton	21,803
Marcus Allen	17,057
Jerry Rice	17,007
Herschel Walker	16,832
Tony Dorsett	16,236

Players of the '90s

Jerry Rice	17,007
Barry Sanders	14,052
Emmitt Smith	12,360
Ricky Watters	7,852
Terrell Davis	3,332

Jerry Rice

Most TDs Scored

Players of the '90s

Jerry Rice	156	Emmitt Smith	115
Jim Brown	126	Barry Sanders	91
Walter Payton	125	Ricky Watters	58
Marcus Allen	125	Terry Allen	58
John Riggins	116	Curtis Martin	32

Trivia Teaser #10

What is the length of the longest field goal in NFL history, and who is the player who holds this record?

Did You Know?

On January 1, 1993, the Houston Oilers were leading the Buffalo Bills 35–0 in the second half of their American Football Conference playoff game, when Buffalo started to get serious. Frank Reich, the Bills' back-up quarterback, threw four touchdown passes as Buffalo gradually caught up to the Oilers and won the game 41–38 in overtime, making this the greatest comeback in NFL history.

Trivia Teaser Answers

#1 **Answer: Footballs are actually made from cow leather.** To meet NFL rules, they are inflated to a pressure of 13 pounds. It remains unclear why footballs are also known as pigskins, but there is one possibility. The game played in England in the twelfth century was called *futballe.* The balls used in this game were inflated pig bladders. Perhaps the name stuck to a game which once really used balls of pigskin.

#2 **Answer: Dan Marino.** Dan plays for the Miami Dolphins. In 1996, Dan Marino became the first quarterback to throw for 50,000 yards in an NFL career. Marino has also thrown more touchdown passes than other top NFL quarterbacks such as John Elway and Jim Kelly. Marino has completed 4,134 passes, about 700 more than Joe Montana and about 2,000 more than either Steve Young or Troy Aikman.

#3 *Answer: Doug Williams.* In 1988 Williams was the quarterback for the Washington Redskins in Super Bowl XXII, when Washington defeated the Denver Broncos 45–10. He was named the game's Most Valuable Player after setting a Super Bowl record by passing for 340 yards. On September 30, 1979, Williams also made history when he played in the first NFL game in which both teams had African American starting quarterbacks. Williams was playing for the Tampa Bay Buccaneers and Vince Evans was quarterback for the Chicago Bears.

Doug Williams

Barry Sanders

#4 *Answer: Barry Sanders.* In the first 8 years of his career with the Detroit Lions, Barry has rushed for 11,725 yards. He is the only running back in NFL history to rush for 1,000 or more yards in each of eight straight seasons. Barry is seventh on the list of the best running backs in NFL history. Among other NFL players of the '90s, only Marcus Allen of the Kansas City Chiefs—who began his NFL career in 1981—has more rushing yards than Sanders.

#5

Answer: The Super Bowl is the annual game between the champions of the National and American Football Conferences, that decides the champion of the National Football League. The first Super Bowl was played in 1967. While it is uncertain where the name, Super Bowl, came from, an exhibit at the Pro Football Hall of Fame in Canton, Ohio, has a possible explanation. Lamar Hunt, owner of the Kansas City Chiefs, says that at first, the Super Bowl was going to be called the Final Game. But Hunt was thinking of changing the name. His children had a toy called a Super Ball. Hunt says, "I may have been thinking about the Super Ball and one day I just happened to come out and call the game the Super Bowl. The name just stuck."

#6

Answer: John Elway of the Denver Broncos. Elway is one of the best quarterbacks in the NFL of the '90s. He led Denver to four Super Bowls—in 1987, 1988, 1990, and 1998, the year the Broncos won. Before beginning his NFL career in 1983, Elway signed a contract in 1981 to play baseball with the New York Yankees. In 1982 the Yankees sent Elway to play for their minor league team in Oneonta, New York. Elway played outfield for the Oneonta Yankees and did very well. But football was Elway's first love, so he decided to give up a baseball career for one in the National Football League.

#7

Answer: Barry Sanders and Emmitt Smith. Sanders has an average of 4.90. His yards gained (11,725) divided by rushing attempts (2,384) = 4.90. This average is the third best in NFL history, behind Jim Brown (5.2) and Joe Perry (5.0). Smith has an average of 4.35, as 10,160 yards gained divided by 2,334 rushing attempts = 4.35.

#8

Answer: A quarterback sack is when the quarterback is tackled behind the line of scrimmage. Deacon Jones, a defensive lineman for the Los Angeles Rams in the 1970s, invented the term "quarterback sack" because he wanted a shorter description than "tackling the quarterback behind the line of scrimmage," which was used before Jones's invention. Deacon Jones was nicknamed the Secretary of Defense because he was such a great defensive player. In 1980 Jones was elected to the Pro Football Hall of Fame, and in 1982 Jones's term, the sack, entered official NFL statistics books.

#9

Answer: Nine of today's 30 NFL teams have never played in the Super Bowl. They are: Seattle Seahawks, Detroit Lions, Houston Oilers, Arizona Cardinals, New Orleans Saints, Atlanta Falcons, Tampa Bay Buccaneers, Carolina Panthers, and Jacksonville Jaguars.

#10

Answer: On November 8, 1970, Tom Dempsey of the New Orleans Saints kicked a 63-yard field goal, the longest in NFL history. Dempsey's kick helped the Saints beat the Detroit Lions 19–17 and also surpassed the previous field goal record by 7 yards. Tom Dempsey was an incredible athlete. He was born with only half of his right foot, his kicking foot. During his football career, Dempsey wore a special kicking shoe over his right foot. He also was born with a deformed right arm. But he overcame his handicaps, became a pro football player, and has a place in the NFL record book. After he kicked his 63-yard field goal, Dempsey was nicknamed the Sledge Hammer because he kicked the ball so hard.

Resources to Check Out

Books

Aylesworth, Thomas G. *The Kids' Almanac of Professional Football.* Cincinnati: Betterway Books, 1992.

Brenner, Richard J. *The Complete Super Bowl Story: Games I-XXII.* New York: East End Publishing, 1987.

Kavanagh, Jack. *Barry Sanders: Rocket Running Back.* Minneapolis: Lerner Publications Company, 1994.

Thornley, Stew. *Emmitt Smith: Relentless Rusher.* Minneapolis: Lerner Publications Company, 1997.

Web site

National Football League homepage: http://www.nfl.com

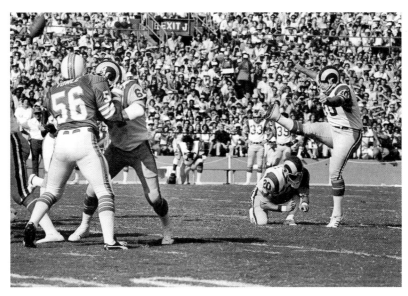

Tom Dempsey kicks a field goal for the Los Angeles Rams.

Bibliography

Hession, Joseph and Kevin Lynch. *War Stories from the Field*. San Francisco: Foghorn Press, 1994.

Horrigan, Joe. *Pioneers of Black Sport: The Early Days of the Black Professional Athlete in Baseball, Boxing and Football*. Northbrook, Ill.: Dodd, Mead, & Co., 1975.

Horrigan, Joe. *The Official Pro Football Hall of Fame Answer Book*. Old Tappan, N.J.: Little Simon, 1990.

Lowry, Philip J. *Green Gridirons. Professional Football* Researchers Association, 1990.

McCloskey, Chris and Chuck Garrity Jr., eds. *1996 National Football League Record & Fact*. New York: Workman Publishing Co., 1996.

Smith, Don R. *Official Encyclopedia of Football*. New York: Gallery Books, 1989.

About the Author

Bruce Adelson is a sports writer, substitute teacher, and former attorney whose published works include *The Minor League Baseball Book.* His work has also appeared in *The Four Sport Stadium Guide* and in publications such as *The Washington Post, Sport Magazine,* and *Baseball America.* The Sports Trivia books are his first children's publications. Adelson lives in Alexandria, Virginia.

About the Illustrator

Harry Pulver Jr. is an illustrator and animator who also plays the accordian and guitar. His work has appeared in numerous national ad campaigns and in books, including *Find It!* and *Tracking the Facts,* two other titles by Lerner Publications.